Simon Watney

FANTASTIC PAINTERS

With 40 color plates

PARK SOUTH BOOKS
An imprint of
Publishers Marketing Enterprises Inc.
386 Park Avenue South
New York, New York 10016

Published by PARK SOUTH BOOKS
An imprint of Publishers Marketing Enterprises Inc.
386 Park Avenue South
New York, New York 10016

First published in the U.K. by
Thames and Hudson Ltd, London

© John Calmann and Cooper Ltd, 1977
This book was designed and produced by
John Calmann and Cooper Ltd, London

Reprinted 1985

Library of Congress Catalog Card Number: 84–61599

ISBN 0–917923–02–2

Printed in Hong Kong by Mandarin Offset Ltd

Introduction

FANTASTIC PAINTING is one of those cultural rag-bag terms that can be used to describe almost any work of art that appears surprising or unusual. Indeed, its very inclusiveness links it to a cluster of terms like 'primitivism' and the 'exotic' with which, as we shall see, it has a great deal in common.

As we look through the illustrations which make up the greater part of this book, it becomes apparent that there are few direct or historical connections between the majority of the painters represented. At the same time we do sense a continuity of some kind. The mere fact that this juxtaposition of images is not uncomfortable, even though they are drawn from such widely different societies and epochs, and painted in such a variety of styles, is remarkable in itself. It is this sense of a unity which we cannot readily explain or understand that I wish to examine in this brief introduction; the unity of that which we describe, for convenience's sake, as fantastic painting.

When looking at paintings, the observer is usually aware of certain categories, or genres, which seem to possess a degree of mutual independence. Such categories have their own distinct histories which, however much they may overlap with one another, can none the less be considered in isolation. At first sight fantastic painting looks like all of these categories, a territory, as it were, that comes to us complete with its own specific history and conventions. But there is no evidence to justify our treating fantastic painting as such an autonomous area. In other words, the term does not refer to a particular 'movement' in art, but rather to a system of taste based upon certain selective principles.

There seem to be certain features which connect the painters included here. These can be divided into four basic areas, each of which is representative of a broad spectrum of fantastic painting, and which I propose to look at individually: images of destruction, Arcadian images, monstrous images, and images of psychological distortion. But first it is necessary to examine the terms 'fantastic painting' and 'fantastic painters' in order to arrive at an understanding of how they are used today and how this curiously vague yet concrete sense of the fantastic came into common currency.

In many ways modern notions of fantastic art depend upon a series of specific, if creative, misunderstandings concerning the art of the past. It is hard, for example, to grasp the precise symbolic meanings of much medieval painting in our materialist age. It is harder still to appreciate the symbolic nature of the culture as a whole, into which such individual meanings fit. Concepts like 'progress' lead us to assume that modern society is more advanced, and that the art of the Middle Ages is simply primitive. It takes a great deal of historical imagination to realize the full implications of the fact that different societies can organize and represent their experience of life in many different ways, which are in no sense inferior to any other, but are simply alternatives. The immediacy and fervour of religious thought which so inform the paintings of Hieronymus Bosch are very alien to contemporary modes of thought. The allegorizing of Giorgione (*plate 3*) or William Blake (*plate 13*), is no longer natural to us.

There is therefore a danger that when describing a particular painting or painter as 'fantastic', we are misinterpreting the original intention. However, the artist's intention is only one concern of the critic, or the spectator. We react strongly to certain painters' work in a singularly consistent way, and those reactions constitute the shape and the 'history', if we may describe it so, of fantastic painting.

This area of painting to which we respond so spontaneously is far larger than any of the individual genres which collectively make up the history of art. Almost any kind of painting may produce examples which could, in this sense, be considered fantastic. But it is always painting which is in some immediately apparent way unconventional. Although the word 'fantastic' has long been one of the terms used to denote the unorthodox and the amazing, our contemporary use of the word is of recent origin.

It comes almost exclusively from the original Surrealist group, founded by André Breton in the early 1920s and characterized by open-mindedness, and hostility to the blinkers of aesthetic orthodoxy. Breton made a distinction between two radically different aspects of Surrealist thought: the 'marvellous' and the 'fantastic'.

For the Surrealists, fantastic art was only one of many subversive strategies designed to manifest their central idea of the marvellous. In Surrealist thought the marvellous signifies every opportunity for revealing the hidden mechanisms of what is felt to be a fundamentally repressive and dehumanizing society. It is seen as a filter through which the entire world might be reconceived, and the artist's function is understood to involve the opening of as many windows as possible on to this domain of Surreality, which is waiting to be released in all of us.

In Surrealist terms, the notion of the fantastic possessed value only as a technique for this changing or raising of consciousness. It was never intended to be an end in itself. In this context the Surrealists rediscovered a range of artists who had been excluded from the traditional accounts of Western Art because they did not fit into the preconceived categories of art history, and it is through their influence that we are aware today of such painters as Arcimboldo and Desiderio.

To a large extent, however, the fantastic element in Surrealism takes the concept of the marvellous at face value, and its celebrity stands in inverse ratio to its significance within the movement as a whole. The fantastic Surrealist painters may present us with images which are often distracting and occasionally hauntingly powerful, but they seem not to have perceived that within the rationalist framework of their culture, the sudden transformations and associations of ordinarily unconnected objects could tend only to reinforce the rigid system they were calling into question. The sight of an apple filling an entire room does not lead us to question our knowledge of the relationship between rooms and apples: its shock is not that of a possibility revealed so much as that of an impossibility reinforced.

The Surrealists' taste for those painters whose work had been traditionally dismissed as eccentric, or even mad, had certain precedents. In the sixteenth century we find allegories whose function was to stimulate speculative thought rather than to illustrate particular moral or philosophic points; such works were described as inventions, or fantasies. The word 'fantasy' as it was then used has little to do with its meaning today, heavy as it is with Freudian connotations, but simply signified the freely operating imagination. By the seventeenth century it had already come to connote a sense of the grotesque or perverse, things fantastical. In this sense it was felt to be the opposite of rational and objective thought.

In the history of taste, the fantastic is a term closely connected to the idea of the sublime. It was seen to exist over and above nature, a highly subjective response to certain evocative, stimulating and melancholy areas of heightened experience. It was thus both the local province of the eighteenth-century Gothic novel and the larger landscape of the Romantic imagination. The fantastic lifted one out of oneself. It was 'rude' and 'horrid'. It suggested visions, hallucinations, and, as such, was not felt to be quite proper. It was the unknown, and for that reason it was both dangerous and seductive. We thus find a certain continuum of usage stretching from the awesome experience of spectacular natural phenomena through to the indulgently subjective musical fantasias of Liszt and Schumann.

In all its contexts, the notion of the fantastic has been applied to situations that stand outside the familiar and reassuring categories by which experience is usually organized. Always it signifies the unusual, the anti-academic, the irrational and the intuitive. It is therefore possible to outline four major areas within the framework of fantastic painting which seem to reflect its major types and directions. All fantastic art employs realistic techniques since it is always concerned to concretize what would otherwise be no more than incoherent feelings or states of mind, and to some extent this simplifies our task of creating order out of apparent chaos.

1. Images of destruction

From Giulio Romano in the sixteenth century (*plate 6*) to John Martin in the nineteenth (*plate 17*), we can detect a certain tradition of disaster images – paintings in which cities, continents and whole worlds are destroyed before our very eyes. This was essentially a function of painting before the days of the cinema, and is a natural extension and exploration of the illusionistic potential of the painter's medium. Apocalyptic visions are in a sense a necessary full-stop at one end of the visionary artist's ability to describe what he sees or imagines. At the same time, the image of the final destruction of the world is a recurring theme in Western consciousness, starting with the Book of Revelations at the end of the New Testament, a text which has preoccupied Christian mystics, and painters, down the ages. It is of course superbly picturesque.

Destruction images are also intrinsically connected to our anxieties concerning death, and reflect a certain morbid temperament which is completely ahistorical. For a devout Christian artist like Bosch (*plate 4*) or Grünewald (*plate 5*), the Last Judgement signified not despair but the sure hope of the world to come after death. Even so, we may detect a lingering fascination with the actual apparatus of annihilation, which is a constant feature of this kind of vision, from the Middle Ages to the Hollywood epic.

In the depiction of such scenes it is also clear that the disillusioned painter could simultaneously exercise his judgement on societies which he felt were depraved or corrupt, or simply indifferent. This element of vicarious enjoyment in the theme of total destruction is often connected to strong, though frustrated, Messianic convictions, as in the cases of Goya (*plate 16*) and Blake (*plate 13*). Such scenes could also be great fun, and there is a parallel stream of images from Desiderio (*plate 10*) to painters such as Danby (*plate 18*), who are witty and almost playful in their handling of such potentially horrifying catastrophes.

2. Arcadian images

The apocalyptic vision finds its complement or necessary opposite in the kind of painting which presents us with a world that either follows such violent punishment, or exists previous to the corruption that occasioned it. Such painting describes an Edenic universe, an ideal world cleansed of ugliness and disorder, conceived on a scale that parallels the sense of goodness which it is intended to represent. This world of paradise gardens and angelic utopias is the other side of the coin, then, to annihilation, and it is not altogether surprising to find that many painters, John Martin for example, were equally obsessed with both. Blake's New Albion stands as the criticism of, and the fantastic substitute for, the horrors of his own nineteenth century.

The Arcadian vision is by its nature panoramic. It is fantasy on the universal scale. Hence the somewhat megalomaniac aspects of Thomas Cole's *Architect's Dream* (*plate 20*) or Signorelli's *Resurrection* (*plate 2*). This is the obsessive quality of excessive conviction. At the same time we find Burne-Jones's *Garden of Pan* (*plate 26*), an innocently erotic domain, located far beyond the taboos and moral rectitude of Victorian England.

Arcadia is traditionally the land beyond history, dreamed of by the frustrated and the repressed; its fantastic qualities exist in strict relation to the degree of frustration and repression felt at any particular time. It is thus a constant theme in European and American art: the pastoral and bucolic world of our most basic dreams and desires.

3. *Monstrous images*

A monster is no more than an unlikely combination of parts gathered from many sources and, as Borges has suggested, the possibility of such permutations borders on the infinite. It is again a fundamental, magical power of the painter to be able to take the natural world to pieces and reconstruct it according to his fantasies.

The monstrous has played a significant part in the history of the Western imagination. The freak was taken as evidence of the Devil's active participation in everyday life. And it is the monster's power to remind us of the limitations of our knowledge of the 'natural' world. The monster signifies the denial of the basic order. Birds with human faces, creatures constructed from many different animal sources – these were seen as the proof of demonic activity and, more simply, they provided artists with a conveniently startling way to illustrate such activity. It is not until our own age that the monster ceases to be a spectacle of terror and becomes instead an object of pity and nostalgia.

Of all the painters included here, it is Arcimboldo who exhibits the most rigorously single-minded fascination with the monstrous. Men and women are conjured out of fruit, fish, trees, vegetables, even loaves of bread. In each of his paintings a very narrow range of materials is expanded into something fantastical (*plate 8*). Clearly such paintings were intended to amaze and shock. They belong to an essentially naive order of art, reminding us of painting's unique power to present us with the impossible and at the same time to inform us of that reality which defines our sense of the possible.

But, as with the fantastic Surrealists, it is a hit or miss affair, and it seems probable that a large part of the effect which such reconjugations of reality have upon us depends upon levels of symbolic meaning and order which lie beyond our ordinary consciousness. This perhaps goes some way to explain the strange innocence and credulity of so many fantastic painters, the mixture of great technical sophistication and almost total conceptional simplicity. Hence the paradox that fantastic art may range, even in a single image, from the most banal allegorizing to expressions of our deepest anxieties, hopes and fears.

4. Psychological distortion

This final category contains a wide range of paintings whose only common feature is that in some way the painter has found something significant or amazing in situations which have few if any intrinsically fantastic features. In each case a metamorphosis has been worked whereby reality has partially given way to something felt or perceived to lie behind it.

Often this takes the form of more or less directly visionary or hallucinatory expression, from Le Douanier Rousseau's haunting picture of the *Sleeping Gipsy* (*plate 29*) and Feininger's *Small Mask* (*plate 37*), to Goya's *Dog* (*plate 16*) and Richard Dadd's *Sketch of an Idea for Crazy Jane* (*plate 19*). Usually in some way sinister or macabre, this kind of fantastic painting ranges from direct expressionism to the great themes of madness and the art of the mad themselves. It affords us glimpses into states of mind which we can share in no other way, and although the results may be subtle, as in Guy Pène Du Bois's *Café du Dôme* (*plate 36*) or Caspar David Friedrich's *Remembrance of Johan Bremer* (*plate 21*), such images tend to lodge in the mind with greater force and influence than other more obviously fantastic spectacles. These are paintings which, once more, affect us below the level of consciousness, playing on doubts and insecurities of which we are largely unaware.

Conclusion

We all have fantasies. In their dreamlike capacity to resolve what would otherwise remain impossible contradictions, the paintings shown and discussed in this book cannot be described as merely consolatory or escapist. For fantasy, like all myth-making, is only one way of describing experience. It may in many cases be the only language available for painters to register their acute sense of a reality which has been lost, or of a reality which is felt to lie beyond the deceptively straightforward surface of appearances.

The appeal of these painters exists partly as a response to the more esoteric aspects of painting in the twentieth century, but this should not lead us to regard them as no more than quaint or bizarre diversions. For it should be apparent that there is a large body of paintings which will always elude the categories and analyses of any completely rationalist approach. Such paintings do belong together in a very real sense, not, as we have seen, to a particular style or movement, but rather as a kind of vertical axis running throughout Western Art, confronting us with what the accounts of that art have ignored.

Such painters present us with an alternative and enigmatic face to our culture. They provide us with a curiously exact mirror of the anxieties and dreams of every epoch. Fantastic art constitutes an imaginative criticism of reality, which functions above all to reflect ourselves, as spectators, revealing all our preconceptions and prejudices, a service which is at once disturbing and provocative.

ANONYMOUS, FLEMISH

1. *The Trinity*

c.1500. Oil on panel. 6½ × 4¼in (16·5 × 10·8cm). Slightly enlarged

This small painting is by an anonymous Flemish artist, working in a highly finished style which establishes him as a follower of the Van Eyck brothers. However fantastic the picture may appear, it should perhaps be regarded as a thoroughly logical, but bizarre, solution to the problem of representing the Christian image of the Trinity, the concept of the indivisible unity of God the Father, the Son, and the Holy Ghost.

USA, private collection

LUCA SIGNORELLI (*c*.1440–1523)

2. *The Resurrection*

c.1500. Fresco. Detail

The frescoes he painted in Orvieto Cathedral between 1499
and 1503 constitute the greatest single achievement in
Signorelli's career. A pupil of Piero della Francesca, he led
his master's style back into the conventions of Gothic art,
whilst retaining a quality of impassive austerity. The
themes of redemption and eternal punishment are treated
in a non-narrative way, the fantastic quality of his work
deriving largely from the literal treatment of his dynamic
medieval subject matter.

Orvieto Cathedral

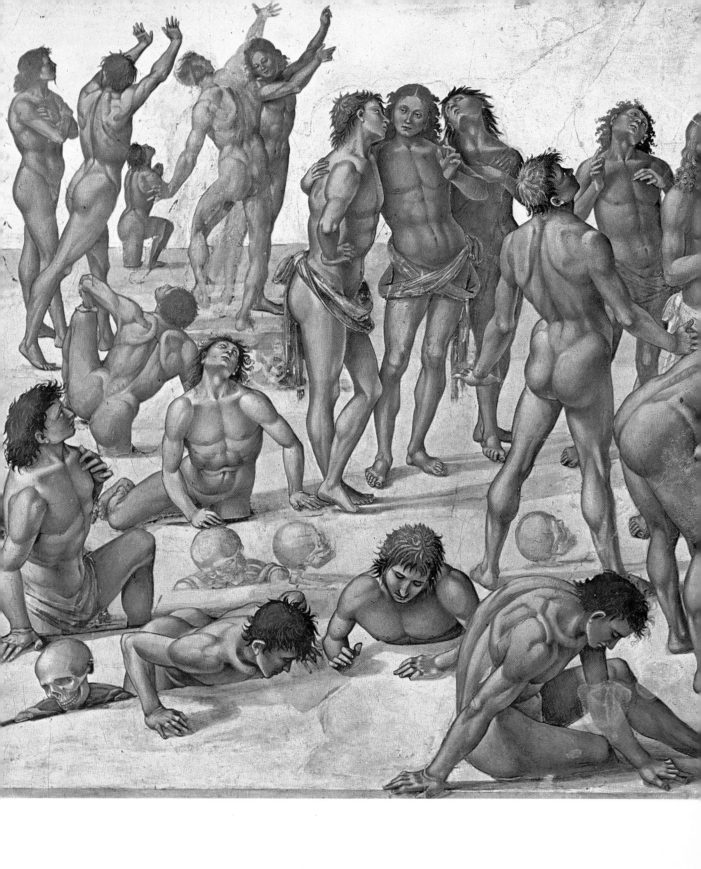

GIORGIONE (1478–1510)

3. *The Tempest*

c.1500. Oil on canvas. 32½ × 28¾in (83 × 73cm)

First recorded in 1530 in an inventory as a 'little landscape
with the tempest with the gipsy and soldier', this remains
one of the most enigmatic paintings in Western art. Edgar
Wind has argued that it contains a precise allegorical
meaning, whereas Lord Clark has seen it as a free fantasy.
Probably the truth lies somewhere between these two
extremes. Whatever meaning was originally intended, it is
clear that this strange scene is replete with poetic and
psychological mystery.

Venice, Accademia Gallery

HIERONYMUS BOSCH (*c.*1450–1516)

4. *The Temptation of St Anthony*

c.1510. Oil on panel. 78 × 46⅞in (194·5 × 119cm). Detail

The bafflingly complex symbolism of Bosch is nowhere more astonishing than in the three-panel altar-piece illustrating scenes in the life of St Anthony, from which this detail is taken. We know that Bosch lived in the small Dutch village of s'Hertogenbosch, where he was born and where he died. This is a late work which was bought after the artist's death by a Portuguese painter, Damiano de Goes.

Lisbon, Museu Nacional de Arte Antiga

MATTHIAS GRÜNEWALD (1470/80–1528)

5. *The Temptation of St Anthony*

c.1515. Oil on panel. Detail

The demonic creatures attacking the fallen figure of St
Anthony come from one of the nine panels which
comprise a large altar-piece painted for a monastic
hospital in Isenheim, a small town on the Franco-German
border. It lies a few miles from the Unterlinden Museum in
which it has been housed for nearly three centuries.
Although Grünewald was clearly influenced by Dürer he
remained an essentially medieval artist, as is apparent in
his passionate and often terrifying expressionism.

Colmar, Unterlinden Museum

GIULIO ROMANO (*c*.1499–1546)

6. *The Hall of the Giants*

c.1530. Fresco

The Palazzo del Tè, of which *The Hall of the Giants* is one
of the great showpieces, was originally intended as an
enormous stable for the horses of the Gonzaga family.
Between 1525 and 1535, however, it was converted into
one of the most magnificent palaces of the High
Renaissance, designed and decorated by Giulio Romano
who had been Raphael's chief studio assistant in Rome.
His frescoes are among the most dazzling illusionistic
spectacles of the sixteenth century.

Mantua, Palazzo del Tè

JACOPO PONTORMO (1494–1557)

7. *Joseph in Egypt*

c.1518. Oil on canvas. 38 × 43⅛in (96·5 × 109·5cm).

Joseph in Egypt is typical of Mannerist painting in its fragmentation of both the narrative and actual picture space. It was painted as one of four pictures to decorate a bridal chamber in the artist's native city of Florence. Vasari states that the figure of the boy seated on a step in the centre foreground is a portrait of the painter Bronzino, then aged about fifteen. *Joseph in Egypt* is the first of Pontormo's many works in which he distorts the classical style of the High Renaissance to bizarre and often expressionistic ends.

London, National Gallery

GIUSEPPE ARCIMBOLDO (1527–1593)

8. *The Gardener*

c.1580. Oil on canvas. 16 × 12in (40·6 × 30·5cm)

Arcimboldo was a Milanese painter attached to the court of the emperors of Austria. He specialized in a highly original form of curiosity picture to attract his aristocratic patrons. *The Gardener* is a typical example of his work, in which a face or whole figure is magically assembled, by the use of a remarkable *trompe l'oeuil* technique, from non-human materials, in this case vegetables.

Cremona, Civic Museum

PIETER BRUEGHEL THE ELDER (*c*.1525–1569)

9. *The Tower of Babel*

1563. Oil on canvas. 44⅞ × 61 in (114 × 155 cm). Detail

The Tower of Babel illustrates the theme of pride which recurs throughout Brueghel's work. He studied in the Low Countries and travelled extensively in Italy in the 1550s, returning to spend the rest of his working life in Brussels and Antwerp. His paintings are largely allegorical and based upon minute observation of natural phenomena, which lends considerable credibility to his vision of the fantastic tower which is described in the Book of Genesis.

Vienna, Kunsthistorisches Museum

MONSÙ DESIDERIO (1593–c.1644)

10. *An Explosion in a Church*

Undated. Oil on canvas. 29⅛ × 39¾in (74 × 101cm)

Very little is known of the artist whose work has been catalogued under the name of Desiderio. It seems likely however that history has rolled together at least two painters, Francesco Desiderio and his close colleague Belisario Corenzio, behind the one name. Desiderio's work is strongly dependent upon northern European Mannerist and Gothic sources, although he worked chiefly in Naples. He specialized in architectural fantasies and visions of an unstable, highly personalized antiquity.

Cambridge, Fitzwilliam Museum

After QUINTEN MASSYS (1465/6–1530)

11. *A Grotesque Old Woman*

c.1510–20. Oil on panel. 25¼ × 17¾in (64 × 45cm)

Massys was a Flemish painter working in Antwerp who was influenced by both Hans Memlinc and Leonardo da Vinci. This painting is closely related to a drawing by da Vinci which is almost certainly a life study. It has been suggested that the subject suffered from an oxycephalic condition. She has been variously identified as Margaret, Duchess of Carinthia and Countess of Tyrol (died 1369), and the Queen of Tunis. It was possibly intended as a piece of social satire – a familiar contemporary theme having been the folly of Vanity.

London, National Gallery

HUBERT ROBERT (1733–1808)

12. *The Spirit of the Tomb*

1795. Oil on canvas. 19¾ × 15in (50 × 38cm)

Hubert Robert was an extremely prolific French painter
who studied at the Academy in Paris and spent much of
his early career in Italy, where he was particularly
receptive to the early Romantic versions of antiquity,
produced by such artists as Pannini and Piranesi. *The
Spirit of the Tomb* belongs to the more melancholy style of
his last years. It shows a young woman seated on the base
of a shattered column, contemplating a sarcophagus. A
winged genius flies overhead bearing a torch, and the
whole scene is dominated by the brooding image of the
pyramid of Cestius.

Paris, Musée des Arts Décoratifs

WILLIAM BLAKE (1757–1827)

13. *The Ghost of a Flea*

c.1819. Tempera on panel. $8\frac{1}{2} \times 6\frac{1}{8}$in (21·6 × 15·5cm)

William Blake was profoundly influenced by both Gothic and High Renaissance painting. His work is mostly of a small scale, even when it is at its most visionary. *The Ghost of a Flea* is related to a series of drawings of 'spirit heads' which he constantly saw around him. It records the memory of a specific demon visitor. Blake explained to his friend Varley that it was the ghost of a flea, 'a spiritualization of the thing', holding a cup of blood and 'whisking' its tongue out of its mouth.

London, Tate Gallery

JEAN-AUGUSTE-DOMINIQUE INGRES (1780–1867)

14. *The Dream of Ossian*

1813. Oil on canvas. 139 × 108in (348 × 275cm)

The epic poetry of the Scot, James Macpherson, which purported to be the work of an ancient Celtic bard, was much in vogue throughout Europe after its translation into French in 1777. Madame de Staël described him as the Homer of the North. *The Dream of Ossian* was painted for another enthusiast, the Emperor Napoleon, to decorate a bedroom in the Palazzo di Monte Cavallo in Rome, which he never actually used. It was taken down in 1815 and bought back by the artist in 1835 to be partly repainted. It shows Ingres in his most overtly Romantic manner.

Montauban, Musée Ingres

JOHANN HEINRICH FUSELI (1741–1825)

15. *Mad Kate*

1806–7. Oil on canvas. 35\frac{3}{4} × 28in (91 × 71cm)

Fuseli was one of the leading figures of the London art world in the late eighteenth century. The son of a Swiss painter, he studied in his native Zurich before coming to England for political reasons in 1763. His paintings dwell on familiar Romantic themes – violence, nightmares, and insanity – but with an hallucinatory intensity which is unrivalled, save by his friend Blake. *Mad Kate* illustrates a poem by William Cowper and shows a servant girl who goes mad upon hearing that her lover has been lost at sea.

Frankfurt am Main, Goethe Museum

FRANCISCO DE GOYA (1746–1828)

16. *The Dog*

1820–3. Fresco, remounted on board

Goya was by far the most important, and the most complex, painter in late eighteenth-century Spain. He worked in a great variety of styles and types of painting, combining fantasy and realism. *The Dog* is one of the so-called Black Paintings, executed in fresco in his home, the Quinta del Sordo, which are often violently expressionistic. It is described in Spanish as 'perro semihundido', the half-submerged dog. It is impossible to be sure what the painting describes.

Madrid, Prado

JOHN MARTIN (1789–1854)

17. *The Destruction of Sodom and Gomorrah*

1852. Oil on canvas. $52\frac{1}{2} \times 82\frac{1}{2}in$ (133·5 × 209·5cm)

John Martin was a native of Northumberland who had trained as a glass painter and been influenced at an early age by seventeenth-century Romantic Italian painters such as Salvator Rosa. A lifelong eccentric and showman, he chose to remain outside the official art establishment of his day. *The Destruction of Sodom and Gomorrah* dates from the last years of his life but was originally conceived as a mezzotint in the late 1830s. It is an entirely characteristic vision of catastrophe and holocaust.

Newcastle upon Tyne, Laing Art Gallery

FRANCIS DANBY (1793–1861)

18. *The Deluge*

1840. Oil on canvas. 112 × 178in (284·5 × 452cm)

Danby was born in Eire and studied in Dublin before
moving to England in 1813, settling in London after
several years spent in Bristol. He fled the country in 1829
after a scandalous marriage and travelled widely on the
Continent. *The Deluge*, a vast allegorical canvas, was
painted to celebrate and advertise his return in 1840.
Although it was not a success, his subsequent work
returns frequently to allegorical and poetic themes, of
which *The Deluge* is in every sense his grandest example.

London, Tate Gallery

RICHARD DADD (1817–1886)

19. *Sketch of an Idea for Crazy Jane*

1855. Watercolour. 14¼ × 10¼in (36 × 26cm)

Dadd trained at the Royal Academy School in London and specialized in minutely observed historical and literary subject matter, treated with great imaginative skill. In 1843 he murdered his father in a fit of madness which has since been diagnosed as paranoid schizophrenia. His insanity did not however affect his capacity to work, and he continued to paint in an extremely idiosyncratic style. *Sketch of an Idea for Crazy Jane* is much simpler than most of Dadd's work. The model is probably one of his fellow inmates at the Bethlem Hospital.

London, Bethlem Royal Hospital and Maudsley Hospital

Sketch of an idea for Crazy Jane.
by Richard Dadd. Bethlehem Hospital. London
September 6th 1855.

THOMAS COLE (1801–1848)

20. *The Architect's Dream*

1840. Oil on canvas. 54 × 84in (137 × 213·5cm)

Cole was an early member of the American 'Hudson River School', and worked extensively in Europe. *The Architect's Dream* was painted for a New Haven architect named Ithiel Town, who eventually refused it. The picture forms a panoramic gazetteer of world architecture from Greece and ancient Egypt to the Italian Renaissance. It belongs to a series of similarly imaginative and poetic paintings, and was shown in London in the 1840s.

Ohio, Toledo Museum of Art

PAINTED BY T. COLE
FOR THE TOWN BROS
1846

CASPAR DAVID FRIEDRICH (1774–1840)

21. *Remembrance of Johan Bremer*

c.1817. Oil on canvas. $17\frac{1}{8} \times 22\frac{1}{2}$in ($43\cdot5 \times 57\cdot2$cm)

Caspar David Friedrich was the most important German painter of the Romantic era. He spent most of his working life in Dresden. His pictures are of a visionary and elegiac nature, often symbolizing the transience of human life. Johan Bremer was a Berlin doctor who died in November 1816. His name appears on the central motif of a gate, which serves, as in many of Friedrich's paintings, as an allusion to death and re-birth. The poplar trees symbolize death and the full moon Christ.

West Berlin, Schloss Charlottenburg, Staatliche Schlösser und Garten

JOHN ANSTER FITZGERALD (1832–1906)

22. *Fairies in a Nest*

Oil on canvas. 9¾ × 12in (25 × 30·5cm)

We know next to nothing of John Anster Fitzgerald
beyond a small body of delicate and often disturbing
paintings. The pictures are tiny, and their size only
serves to exaggerate the scale of the birds and little
animals which seem huge in contrast to the fairies and
elfin figures with whom they usually appear. *Fairies in a
Nest* is particularly unnerving since the construction of the
painted nest is extended out into the elaborately
constructed frame.

London, Maas Gallery

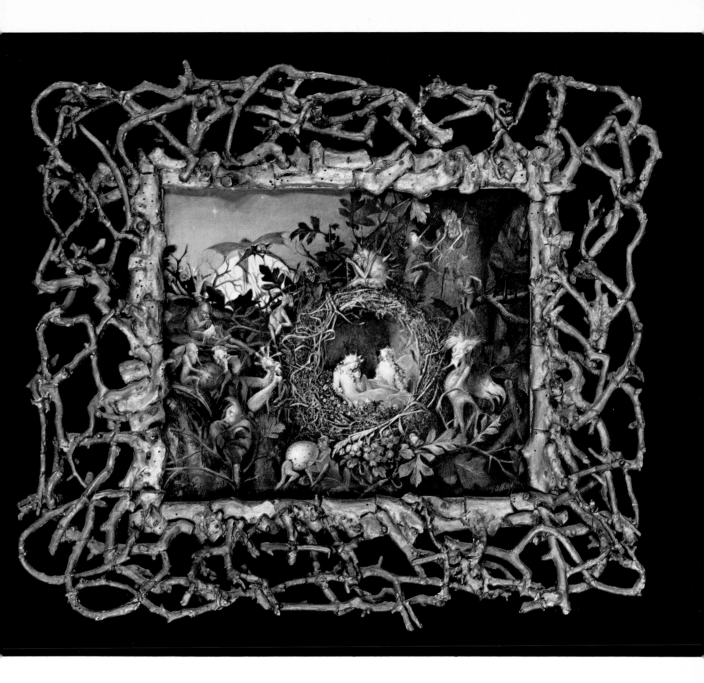

GUSTAVE MOREAU (1826–1898)

23. *Fleur Mystique*

c.1875. Oil on canvas. 99$\frac{3}{4}$ × 54in (253 × 137cm)

Much of Moreau's later work remains unfinished and the *Fleur Mystique* presents us with a dramatic contrast between the freely brushed-in Leonardo-esque landscape, and the detailed hieratic figure of the Virgin Mary enthroned upon an enormous lily, which is fed by the blood of saints and martyrs. It is entirely in character that Moreau, the most celebrated of the French Symbolists, should take so pagan and ambiguous an approach to such a central Christian image.

Paris, Musée Gustave Moreau

ODILON REDON (1840–1916)

24. *The Winged Man, or The Fallen Angel*

1890. Oil on canvas. 17¼ × 14¼in (44 × 36cm)

Odilon Redon was an extreme recluse who took up oil painting after some twenty years working as a draughtsman and lithographer. He wrote in a celebrated phrase that he wanted to place the logic of the visible in the service of the invisible. *The Winged Man* depicts a recurrent motif in his work. Fragments from many different myths and legends are reassembled into a new and mysterious whole which defies any single specific interpretation.

Bordeaux, Musée des Beaux-Arts

ARNOLD BÖCKLIN (1827–1901)

25. *The Mermaid*

1886/7. Tempera on panel. $40\frac{1}{2} \times 59\frac{3}{8}$in (103 × 150cm)

Böcklin was a Swiss-born painter who studied in Germany
and Paris before settling in Rome in 1850. His work is
highly Romantic in mood and influenced both the
Symbolists and the Expressionists. He constantly sought
allegorical ways of depicting fear and isolation, themes
that often recur in his work. *The Mermaid* is one of a
number of paintings on the same subject.

Berne, Kunstmuseum

SIR EDWARD BURNE-JONES (1833–1898)

26. *The Garden of Pan*

1886/7. Oil on canvas. $60\frac{3}{8} \times 73\frac{5}{8}$ in ($152 \cdot 5 \times 187$ cm)

For over a decade Burne-Jones had planned to paint a picture of the beginning of the world as a reaction to the 'dazzle of London wit and wisdom'. *The Garden of Pan*, a strangely soft and gently erotic landscape, shows the artist's familiar idyllic dream world, but unusually bare of the symbolic trappings of late Pre-Raphaelitism.

Melbourne, National Gallery of Victoria

GIOVANNI SEGANTINI (1858–1899)

27. *The Punishment of Luxury*

1891. Oil on canvas. 39 × 68in (99 × 172·8cm)

Segantini was a Milanese painter who combined an interest in Pointillism with a fundamentally Symbolist outlook. Many of his pictures derive however from Buddhist sources, in which he was very interested. *The Punishment of Luxury* is typical of his tendency to personify his own somewhat unorthodox ethical beliefs within a loosely religious framework.

Liverpool, Walker Art Gallery

GEORGE FREDERIC WATTS (1817–1904)

28. *Dweller in the Innermost*

1886. Oil on canvas. $41\frac{3}{4} \times 27\frac{1}{2}in$ (106 × 70cm)

Watts was a leading English Symbolist painter in the late nineteenth century. He was a reserved, mystical, melancholic man. The figure of the *Dweller in the Innermost* holds a silver trumpet of truth, which symbolizes conscience. The painter himself suggested that no single interpretation of the picture could be made, referring to its ideas as vague murmurings which kept him from his work.

London, Tate Gallery

HENRI ROUSSEAU (1844–1910)

29. *The Sleeping Gipsy*

1897. Oil on canvas. 51 × 79in (129 × 200·7cm)

Rousseau was a Parisian customs officer who would have
liked naively to have been recognized as a conventional
Salon painter. *The Sleeping Gipsy* was painted in 1897 and
was exhibited in that year at the Salon des Indépendants.
He later offered it to his home town of Laval in a letter to
the mayor, who refused it. He described it as a picture of a
wandering negress, worn out by fatigue, who is detected
by a lion which refrains from devouring her. There is an
effect of moonlight, very poetic.

New York, Museum of Modern Art

PAUL KLEE (1879–1940)

30. *The Golden Fish*

1925. Oil on cardboard. 19½ × 27¼in (49·6 × 69·1cm)

Much of Klee's early work is characterized by fantastic images which were intended to function as metaphors for his states of mind. From Redon, Blake and Goya he went on to study Cézanne and Picasso, but always in the context of his search for means to express his inner life through colour. *The Golden Fish* shows him at his most lyrical and gently mysterious.

Hamburg, Kunsthalle

MAX ERNST (1891–1976)

31. *The Anti-Pope*

1941/2. Oil on canvas. 63 × 50in (160 × 127cm)

Max Ernst was a self-taught artist who was instrumental in the formation of both the Cologne Dada group and the Parisian Surrealist group. As a painter he pioneered a number of new techniques which were intended to challenge our ordinary responses to the natural world in order to reveal the existence of a hidden and alternative order. *The Anti-Pope* belongs to a series of pictures dealing with the theme of metamorphosis and transformation. It was painted at the time of his marriage to Peggy Guggenheim.

Venice, Peggy Guggenheim collection

RENÉ MAGRITTE (1898–1967)

32. *The Rape*

1934. Oil on canvas. 28 × 21¼in (73 × 54cm)

Magritte was a Belgian painter who began to paint in a
Surrealist manner, combining objects and parts of objects
in a wholly irrational manner. He worked briefly in Paris
in the late 1920s but soon left the Surrealist group since he
did not agree with many of their tenets. Much of his work
expresses a curious mixture of admiration and disgust at
ordinary middle-class life. *The Rape* is his first version of a
theme to which he often returned, the analagous
relationship between the human torso and the face. His
titles are usually poetic allusions rather than accurate
descriptions of his paintings.

USA, private collection

SALVADOR DALI (1904–)

33. *The Enigma of William Tell*

1933. Oil on canvas. 86⅝ × 137¾in (220 × 350cm)

The Enigma of William Tell is one of Dali's most sinister paintings. Much of his work from the early 1930s explores the fantastic possibilities of organ transplants and obsessive sexual distortions. As a founder member of the Surrealist group, Dali was interested in the re-ordering of reality, together with his own somewhat self-conscious erotic fantasies.

Stockholm, Modern Museum

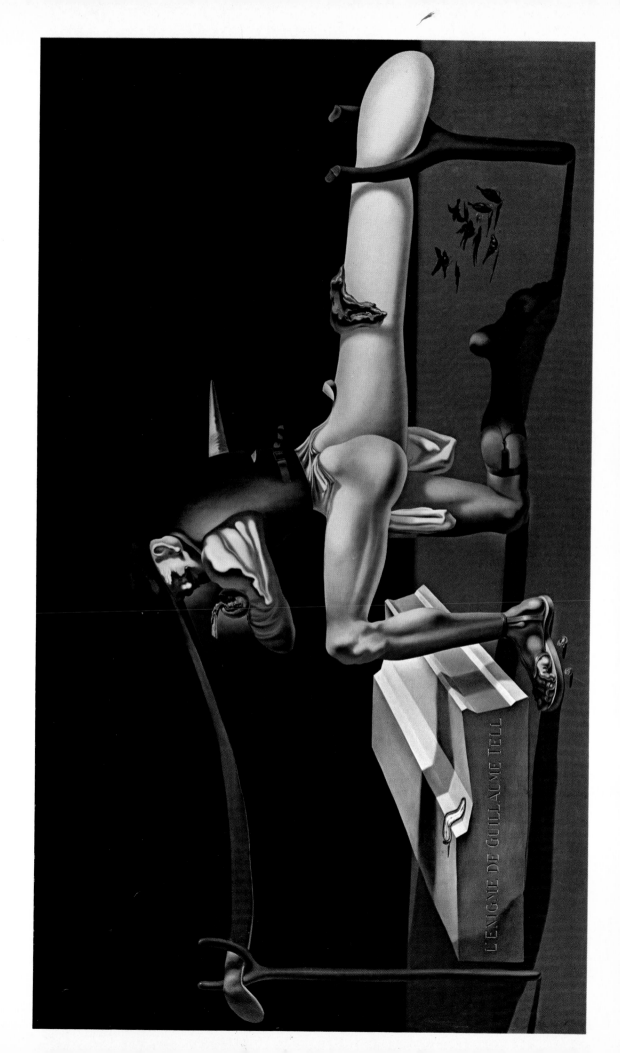

PAUL DELVAUX (1897–)

34. *Venus Asleep*

1944. Oil on canvas. $68\frac{1}{8} \times 78\frac{3}{8}$in (173 × 199cm)

Delvaux is a Belgian painter who was deeply influenced by Magritte and de Chirico in the late 1930s. Most of his pictures depict female nudes surrounded by classical architecture. *Venus Asleep* was painted in Brussels during attacks by flying bombs towards the end of the Second World War. He has written that he hoped to contrast the drama and anguish of that situation with the calm of Venus. There is certainly a mood of strange disquiet around the figure of the sleeping goddess, watched over by a black dressmaker's dummy and a skeleton.

London, Tate Gallery

LUIGI RUSSOLO (1885–1947)

35. *Music*

1911. Oil on canvas. 86 × 53½in (219·7 × 135·9cm)

Russolo was a founder member of the Italian Futurist
movement which sought, under the influence of the
French writer Henri Bergson, to produce equivalents, in
painting, to our sense of movement and time. In Russolo's
case this also involved an attempt to convey the
perception of sound and smell. *Music*, then, was intended
to express the duration of a piece of music. This actually
led him to experiment with the idea of a Futurist music.

London, Mr and Mrs Eric Estorick collection

GUY PÈNE DU BOIS (1884–1958)

36. *Café du Dôme*

1926. Oil on panel. 217½ × 181¼in (552 × 461cm)

Du Bois was a Brooklyn-born painter and art critic who studied in Paris early in the century, returning to the New York School of Art under Robert Henri. This picture shows a scene in the famous Parisian café. It is painted with a mixture of realism and fantastic simplification of forms which gives his women a strangely disembodied, doll-like appearance.

Washington, National Gallery of Art

LYONEL FEININGER (1871–1956)

37. *The Small Mask*

1936. Oil on canvas. $18\frac{7}{8} \times 15\frac{3}{4}$in (48 × 40cm)

Feininger's *Small Mask* dates from the artist's last year in Germany before his departure for the United States after his paintings had been officially condemned by the National Socialists as 'degenerate'. He taught at the Bauhaus from 1919 until its enforced closure in 1933. Feininger was of a more openly mystical temperament than most of his Bauhaus colleagues, and *The Small Mask* reflects the meditative symbolic direction which he followed in the 1930s.

London, Marlborough Gallery

STANLEY SPENCER (1891–1959)

38. *The Centurion's Servant*

1914. Oil on canvas. 45 × 45in (114·5 × 114·5cm)

Stanley Spencer was an English painter of predominantly religious and imaginative subjects. *The Centurion's Servant* derives from three distinct sources: firstly the Biblical story of the faithful centurion; secondly a story his mother told him about villagers in his native Cookham praying for the recovery of a dying man; lastly the memory of a female servant's bedroom in his parents' house which, as a child, he had been forbidden to enter. The painting shows this room, together with the artist and members of his family.

London, Tate Gallery

R. B. KITAJ (1932–)

39. *The Man of the Woods and the Cat of the Mountains*

1973. Oil on canvas. 60 × 60in (152·5 × 152·5cm)

Kitaj was born in the United States but came to live in England in 1958. His work is concerned with human relationships and a sense of the marvellous in everyday life which distinguishes him as, to some extent, an inheritor of Surrealism. *The Man of the Woods and the Cat of the Mountains* derives from an anonymous nineteenth-century engraving of the same name, and it explores a characteristically mysterious situation. Kitaj sees it as an idyllic painting. The man's head is based upon that of George Sand; the cat is made up.

London, Tate Gallery

DAVID HOCKNEY (1937–)

40. *Picture emphasizing Stillness*

1962. Oil and Letraset on canvas. 72 × 60¼in (183 × 153cm)

Hockney's *Picture emphasizing Stillness* belongs to a series
of pictures which runs throughout his career in which the
familiar and the fantastic are juxtaposed. The two men
belong to the safe world of the small house on the right,
whose space is dramatically invaded by the leaping
leopard. A Letraset text reads 'They are perfectly safe. This
is a still.'

London, Kasmin Gallery

SIMON WATNEY AND BLACKER CALMANN COOPER LIMITED *would like to thank the museums and owners for allowing works from their collections to be reproduced. Plates 7 and 11 are reproduced by courtesy of the Trustees of the National Gallery, London; Plate 10 by permission of the Syndics of the Fitzwilliam Museum, Cambridge; Plate 19 by courtesy of the Board of Governors of The Bethlem Royal Hospital & The Maudsley Hospital; Plate 26 by permission of the National Gallery of Victoria, Melbourne (Felton Bequest, 1919); and Plate 31 by permission of the Collection, the Museum of Modern Art, New York (Gift of Mrs Simon Guggenheim). Plate 32 is reproduced by courtesy of Madame Magritte, Plate 34 by courtesy of Paul Delvaux, Plate 38 by permission of the executors of the estate of Sir Stanley Spencer, and Plate 39 by courtesy of R. B. Kitaj. Plate 33 is © by ADAGP Paris 1977, Plate 35 © by SPADEM Paris 1977, and Plate 37 © by ADAGP Paris & Cosmopress Geneva 1977. Transparencies were provided by Scala (Plates 2, 3, 6, 8 and 14), the Cooper-Bridgeman Library, London (Plate 4), Photographie Bulloz (Plate 23), John Webb (Plates 28, 34, 38), The Arts Council of Great Britain (Plate 32), and the Marlborough Gallery, London (Plates 37 and 39).*